Cornelius H. Edgar

The Curse of Canaan Rightly Interpreted

and kindred topics - three lectures delivered in the Reformed Dutch

Church, Easton, Pa. - January and February, 1862

.

.

Cornelius H. Edgar

The Curse of Canaan Rightly Interpreted
*and kindred topics - three lectures delivered in the Reformed Dutch Church, Easton,
Pa. - January and February, 1862*

ISBN/EAN: 9783337302764

Printed in Europe, USA, Canada, Australia, Japan

Cover: Foto ©Lupo / pixelio.de

More available books at **www.hansebooks.com**

THE CURSE OF CANAAN

RIGHTLY INTERPRETED,

AND

KINDRED TOPICS.

THREE LECTURES,

DELIVERED IN THE

REFORMED DUTCH CHURCH, EASTON, PA.

JANUARY AND FEBRUARY, 1862.

BY THE PASTOR,

Rev. CORNELIUS H. EDGAR.

NEW YORK:

BAKER & GODWIN, PRINTERS,

Printing-House Square, opposite City Hall.

1862.

LECTURE I.

THE CURSE OF CANAAN:—BY WHOM AND ON WHOM PRONOUNCED.

———•◆•———

GENESIS IX., 24, 25: And Noah awoke from his wine, and knew what his younger son had done unto him. And he said, Cursed be Canaan; a servant of servants shall he be unto his brethren.

THOSE who derive from these words divine authority for enslaving the Negro, are bound to show that Noah spoke these words *as he was moved by the Holy Ghost.* They are also bound to show that the *Negro is descended from Canaan.*

It is not in this passage, nor is it anywhere, in the inspired writings, declared, that Noah uttered these words by the authority and inspiration of God.

An argument has been built upon these words to excuse and to justify the enslaving of the descendants of Ham. In the argument it is assumed that " God spake all these words." It is only an assumption. It must be proved that Noah uttered them when inspired, and by command and authority of the Almighty. For if, when Noah cursed Canaan—as we have no doubt he did curse Canaan—he was speaking as a *private* person, and not as an inspired prophet of Jehovah, no inference as to the divine institution of slavery can be therefrom derived.

You are not to suppose that " holy men of old, who spake as they were moved by the Holy Ghost," were *always*, and in all things, moved by the Holy Ghost. Sometimes they spoke as other men. I raise the question,—*Did Noah utter his curse on Canaan as he was moved by the Holy Ghost?* Necessity is laid upon those who infer, from Noah's curse upon Canaan, that God instituted slavery, to show, without a shadow of a doubt, from the Bible, as the only admissible authority in the case, that Noah was speaking at the time *by authority.* Unlesss it can be proved, either by a direct affirmation or by a fair inference, that he did so speak, then, the premises as to the divine institution of slavery being unsound, the inference is not legitimate. I am entirely honest in doubting whether Noah was under special inspiration when he said, " Cursed be Canaan." This doubt I can entertain without invalidating my conviction that Noah was, upon the whole, righteous before God; and that, as a preacher, he labored for more than a century to reform a corrupt church, and to save a sinful and doomed generation. I am confirmed in my doubt when I read that God commended him before the flood, while I find no special commendation of him after the flood. When I read of Noah's sad fall, after he began to be an husbandman—being drunken—I then see a force in the little word *this,* in Chap. vii. 1, which had escaped my notice until I see the emphasis which Noah's subsequent history has given it; for in that place God says, "Thee have I seen righteous before me in *this* generation?" whereas in a subsequent generation Noah was not so faultless, and fell below Shem and Japheth in moral deportment.

What a sad and instructive history of the second progenitor of the human family is contained in the last ten verses of the ninth chapter of Genesis! The great Noah, missionary of the Lord, perhaps to the ends of the earth, has left his high calling. He has gone down from the high position of being a preacher, and has planted a vineyard. And what next? The most natural thing to think of. He drank of the wine. And what then? Just what has happened to ten thousand who drink wine,— he *was drunken.* And what then? He was humbled and disgraced in the presence of his family and before all the world to the end of time. What a fall! He has laid aside preaching; for not a word do we find has he uttered as a preacher since the flood. God has left him to worldliness and its results. Immediately upon recovering from his drunkenness, what does he say? Discovering the misconduct of Canaan, his grandson (his younger son), who was either the discoverer and publisher of Noah's shame, or the conniver with Ham in publishing it, Noah, as was most natural, moved by chagrin and indignation and self-reproach, and not moved by the Holy Ghost, says, Canaan deserves to be a menial servant for his mean and undutiful exposure of my shame. It was just as natural, without any special inspiration, for him to offer an opinion and to express his wishes as to the future history of Japheth and Shem, whose conduct he could not but commend.

It is not necessary—nay, it is not admissible—to take the words of Noah, as to Shem and Japheth, as *prophetic*. We shall presently see that, as prophetic, they have failed. Let us not, in expounding Scripture, introduce the *supernatural* when the *natural* is adequate. Noah had now known the peculiarities of his sons long enough, and well enough, to be able to make some probable conjecture as to their future course, and their success or failure in life. Is is what parents do now-a-days. They say of one son, He will succeed,—he is so dutiful, so economical, so industrious. They say of another, This one will make a good lawyer—he is so sharp in an argument. Of another, they say, We will educate him for the ministry, for he has suitable qualifications. While of another they may be constrained to predict that he will not succeed, because he is indolent, and selfish, and sensual. Does it require special inspiration for a father, having ordinary common sense, to discover the peculiar talents and dispositions of his children, and to predict the probable future of each of them? Sometimes they hit it; sometimes they miss it. Shall it not be conceded to Noah that he could make as probable a conjecture, as to his sons, as your father made as to you, or as you think yourselves competent to make for either of your sons? Noah made a good hit. What he said as to the future of his sons, and of their posterity, has turned out, in some respects, as he said it would, but *not exactly*,—not so exactly as to authorize our calling his words an inspired prophecy, as we shall presently show. But, if we set out to establish or to justify slavery upon these words of Noah, on the assumption GOD *spake* by Noah as to the curse and blessings here recorded, we have a right to expect to find the facts of history to correspond. If the facts of history do not correspond with these words of Noah, then God did not speak them by Noah as his own. Let us face this matter. It is said, by those who interpret the curse of Canaan as divine authority for slavery, that *God has hereby ordained that the descendants of Ham shall be slaves.* The descendants of Shem are not, of course, doomed to that curse. Now, upon the supposition that these are the words of God, and not the denunciations of an irritated father just awaking from his drunkenness, we ought not to find *any of Canaan's descendants out of a condition of slavery, nor any of the descendants of Shem in it.* If we do, then either these are not God's words, or God's words have not come true. But it is a fact that not all of Ham's entire descendants, nor even of Canaan's descendants (on whom *alone,* and not *at all on Ham,* nor on his *three other sons,* Noah's curse fell), are now, *nor ever have been,* as a whole, in a state of bondage. The Canaanites were not slaves, but free and powerful tribes, when the Hebrews entered their territory. The Carthagenians, it is generally admitted, were descended from Canaan. They certainly were free and powerful when, in frequent wars, they contended, often with success, against the formidable Romans. If the curse of Noah was intended for all the descendants of Ham, it signally failed in the case of the first military hero mentioned in the Bible, who was the founder of a world-renowned city and empire. I refer to Nimrod, who was a son of Cush, the oldest son of Ham. Of this Nimrod the record is, "He began to be a mighty one in the earth: he was a mighty hunter before the Lord: and the beginning of his kingdom was Babel, and Erech, and Accad, and Calneh, in the land of Shinar. Out of that land went forth Asshur and builded Nineveh, and the city Rehoboth, and Calah, and Resen, between Nineveh and Calah; the same is a great city." This is Bible authority, informing us that the grandson of Ham (Nimrod, the son of Cush) was a mighty man—*the great man* of the world, in his day—the founder of the Babylonian empire, and the ancestor of the founder of the city of Nineveh, one of the grandest cities of the ancient world. We are not led to conclude, from these wonderful achievements by the posterity of Cush (who was the progenitor of the Negroes), that this line of Ham's descendants were so *weak in intellect* as to be unable to set up and maintain a government.

Again : on the assumption that, according to the curse on Canaan, Ham's descendants are doomed to bond-service, and Shem's descendants are to be blessed with the position and privilege of having slaves from the progeny of Ham, we have a right to expect to find the facts in history to correspond. Certainly, before consulting history, we shall not expect to find Shem's children in bondage, if God has said Canaan shall be Shem's slave. An apologist for slavery as a divine institution (Servitude, p. 9) says, "We find in times past the prophetic declarations of the Patriarch Noah have been fulfilled, and that the curse and blessing extend to our day, and are still in process of fulfillment, according to God's sure word." This writer quotes the venerable Dr. Mede as saying, "There never has been a son of Ham who has shaken a sceptre over the head of Japheth. Shem has subdued Japheth, and Japheth has subdued Shem ; but Ham has never subdued either." I would say to this apologist, it is not as he and Dr. Mede represent it. He is ignorant of history, or he willfully misrepresents it. It is astonishing that Dr. Mede should have said what is ascribed to him—"Ham never subdued either !" Shem never in bondage ! Has Dr. Mede never read that the Hebrews were in bondage in Egypt hundreds of years ? Egypt was the country of *Mis-raim*, the second son of Ham. The Hebrews were Shemites. Shemites were in slavery, and Hamites were their masters. "Melchizedek, whose name was expressive of his character— *king of righteousness* (or a righteous king)—was a worthy priest of the most high God; and Abimelech, whose name imports *parental king*, pleaded the integrity of his heart and the righteousness of his nation before God, and his plea was admit-ted. Yet, both these personages appear to have been Canaan-ites."—(*Bush.*) Melchizedek and Abimelech—*Canaanites*— among the most honorable names in sacred history ! Consider how great Melchizedek (a Canaanite) was, unto whom even the princely Abraham (a Shemite) gave the tenth of the spoils ! " Nimrod went to Asher, and built Nineveh ;" and this he could not have accomplished if he had not first subdued the descendants of Shem. Consider how great Nimrod—a *Cushite*—a *Hamite*—was, who shook a sceptre over the Shemites, and took their country! Thus we see that these words of Noah, if you attempt to apply them to the history of the branches of his family, are not verified in history. But God's word of prophecy cannot fail. Therefore Noah's curse on Canaan, and predictions as to Shem and Japheth, are his *guess*, founded, in part, by a knowledge of his children, and prompted as much by his incensed feelings. We cannot, in the light of history, receive these words as uttered by Noah when *moved by the Holy Ghost*, but as the hasty malediction of an incensed father, irritated both by his drunkenness and a feeling of indignation against that member of the family who had exposed his shame. · It is not a pleasant duty thus to hold up the fall of our father, Noah. We desire not to do it in the spirit of Ham and Canaan. But we are in search of the truth, with a view to refute the perversion of the Scriptures by the oppressors of our fellow-men. There is additional proof that the curse and blessings in the 25th, 26th, 27th verses of the 9th chapter of Genesis, were *Noah's*, and not *Jehovah's*. In the first verse of this chapter, "God blessed Noah and his sons." Notice, it is—God blessed *all the sons* of Noah. But in these verses under consideration, we read it was NOAH—not God—who said, "Cursed be Canaan;" at the same time repeating, in substance, that Japheth and Shem had the Lord's blessing, and his own good wishes and expectations that they would do better in their own and in their family history than Canaan. It really seems that Noah had taken the responsibility of revoking the Lord's blessing, in part, which had been pronounced on *all his sons alike*. It is quite probable that slavery was at this time instituted, not by divine authority, but by parental authority,—*i. e.*, by Noah, in the spirit of revenge on Canaan. It is not improbable that this member of the family was from that time subject to the contempt and tyranny and oppression of his grandfather and uncles and cousins and brothers. It served him right, if it was so. It was a righteous retribution of God, for dishonoring the venerable Noah. But God's *providence* is not the same thing as a *divine institution*, or an *inspired prophecy*.

The curse on Canaan and the blessing on Shem is the word of the Lord, or it is not. If it be the word of the Lord, it could not have failed. But that word *has failed;* therefore, it is *not the word of the Lord.* If it be not the word of the Lord, no justification of slavery can be argued from this famous passage of Scripture.

But this passage of Scripture is the grand foundation for a scriptural vindication of the right to hold human beings in bondage. It is to the curse of Canaan that slavery among the Hebrews is traced, and by this justified, in the arguments of those who defend slavery as a divine institution. One writer, who may be supposed to speak for all of his class, quotes Lev. xxv., 44-46: "Both thy bondmen and thy bondmaids which thou shalt have, shall be of the heathen that are round about you; of them shall ye buy bondmen and bondmaids." And then remarks, "We do not consider these texts, or this permission, as a foundation of their right to hold these heathen as bondmen and bondwomen forever. We consider this portion of Scripture as containing a new writ or warrant of execution, for the services of the Canaanites, issued to Moses and the children of Israel by the great Judge of the earth, upon the judgment rendered in the days of Noah, 850 years before." But if the foundation is laid in the *sand,* what will become of the house? "The earth stands upon a turtle," is the doctrine of the Hindoo cosmogony. Yes; but what does the turtle stand upon? American slavery is justifiable, because Paul recognized slavery as an institution existing in the Roman empire. Slavery was justifiable among the Romans because it existed among the Hebrews. Slavery among the Hebrews was scriptural and right because an irritated father, just recovering from his drunkenness, cursed one particular member of the family for his improper behavior! ! This is the argument. But if the foundations of slavery be destroyed, what shall the *righteous* (? ?) defenders of the patriarchal *institution* (? ?) do? Noah's curse was not the authorized utterance of God, as we have shown, 1st, from the fact that it is not said that *the Lord spake unto Noah,* saying, "Cursed be Canaan;" and, 2d, because the *programme* laid down as to the curse and blessings on Canaan and Shem has not been carried out.

An objection to my argument may be attempted. It would probably be stated thus: *If God, by Moses, ordains certain statutes as to slavery,—what is this but a* DIVINE INSTITUTION, *authorizing the holding of human beings in unwilling* SERVI-TUDE?

The answer is simple and conclusive. We say, it does not follow that, because God ordains certain laws as to slavery, therefore he *instituted* and *approves* the enslaving of human beings. Let us premise—1st, When wise, patient, and far-seeing legislators, founders of states, and reformers, cannot accomplish the best thing conceivable or desirable, they aim to accomplish the next best thing possible; 2d, Regulating an existing custom is not to be confounded with instituting or approving it; 3d, Moses was the inspired legislator for the HEBREWS, and not the modeler of constitutions for other states and other times. These premises are impregnable. The application of these premises to the case in hand is the answer to those who justify American slavery on the ground that God, by Moses, ordained certain statutes as to slavery among the Hebrews. Moses, although an inspired legislator, had a previously fixed social element with which to deal. Slavery existed at the time. It had been for centuries the system of labor among the Egyptians, from whom the Hebrews had just escaped. The Hebrews would naturally think that they, just setting up for themselves as one of the nations of the earth, and having slaves, must *continue* that system of labor. Moses, proceeding on the principle of doing the best thing possible under the circumstances, accedes to their demand so far as to lay down certain rules regulating slavery. Divorce was a custom among the Hebrews. Moses allowed men to put away their wives. Did Moses institute and approve of divorce? The divine law of marriage is that a man can have but one wife at a time, and that only one kind of offence is a sufficient reason for divorce. And yet Moses allowed men to put away their wives. Their hearts were so hard that he saw the women would suffer from the cruel treatment of their husbands if he abruptly discontinued divorce. To disallow divorce is the law of God, and, of course, the best thing conceivable; but, under the circumstances, it was not possible or expedient to put the rule in force. Moses chose the less evil. At a later day in Jewish history, Samuel assents, under protest, to a change of the form of government. The people demanded to have a king. It was not best for them, in his judgment, and yet he anoints a king. The question, to the candid, is, Did Samuel approve of the Hebrews having a monarchical government? Certainly not ; and yet he anointed their king, and gave them a written constitution. He was directed by God to do it. Did Moses institute and sanction divorce? Certainly not. He found it existing. It existed throughout the East. It had existed among their forefathers. They were not prepared to have it annulled ; and so Moses *allowed* certain customs as to divorce, not instituting or approving, but *regulating* these things. Our Savior seems to sanction what Moses did. The reasoning is precisely parallel as to slavery. Moses, under authority from God, lays down certain rules as to slavery. It was the best thing that could be done. Was this instituting or sanctioning slavery? If it was, then Moses, under authority from God, instituted and sanctioned divorce,—and Samuel, under authority from God, authorized and approved the monarchy.

It is easy to understand this method of overturning the baseless fabric of the argument for slavery derived from the statutes of Moses, by the treatment of a dissipated son by loving and patient parents. Suppose the profligate boy comes home late at night, drunk, and cold, and noisy—suppose this is a confirmed habit—suppose his loving mother waits for his coming, depriving herself of sleep, and welcomes him with a smile and warm refreshments—suppose the father tells him he must fasten the door as he comes in, and must not disturb the family with his noise. Are not these the considerate acts and rules of the parents as to the dissipated habits of a boy whose heart is fully set in him to continue his evil ways? These are regulations and usages of the family, which recognize the drunken habits of a son, who is dear to his doating parents, notwithstanding his wicked ways. Is it a fair inference that these parents *trained* that boy to his present courses, or that they instituted drunkenness as a rule of their house, or that they connive at or approve or encourage him in his ways? I might add to this supposed case the directions of the father, who pays the bills which his son contracts, that he must not drink bad whiskey, but good wine, and that he must not buy it of A. B., but of C. D., if he will get drunk. And still, even with these additional regulations, I cannot infer that the course of this profligate is approved. Neither can it be inferred that, because God gave laws regulating slavery among a people persisting in having, and who, he foresaw, would persist in having, the same system of labor that the heathen nations had, therefore God instituted slavery; and, therefore, we may exact, without their consent and without requital, the labor of our fellow-men.

There is another difficulty in which the apologist for slavery is involved who intrenches himself behind the statutes of Moses on this subject. It is by him forgotten that whilst Moses was the revealer of the moral law for all mankind, he was the founder of the HEBREW Commonwealth. As the revealer of the moral law, his words are for all mankind. As the founder of the Hebrew Commonwealth, his mission was to the Hebrews alone. The regulations as to slavery were a part of the *civil code*. If it is argued that the enactments of this civil code authorize slavery for all other nations, then two results follow. *First*. Slavery must be a part of every system of civil law. *Second*. The ceremonial law as to sacrifices, and circumcision, and pilgrimages to Jerusalem, is binding upon those who derive authority for slavery from the civil law enacted by Moses expressly for the Hebrews. The argument for justifying slavery, because the civil code which Moses gave the Hebrews recognized and regulated slavery, proves too much. If it be divine authority for other nations to hold human beings in bondage, does it not do more than permit it? Does it not enjoin it? If we accept one of these institutes of Moses as to matters not pertaining to the moral law, how can we consistently decline all the others? If we take slavery because God has ordained certain rules as to an existing system of labor, we must take the whole code with it—tithing, sacrifices, circumcision, rights of primogeniture, divorce, and all.

Having shown that slavery has no foundation in the curse pronounced on Canaan, considered as the *uninspired* word of Noah (he not even pretending to speak by authority of God), we are willing, for the sake of examining the argument, *now to consider the text as the inspired word of God uttered by Noah as to Canaan.* It is by many—even by all, so far as I know—thus considered, received, and interpreted. Let us so receive it, for argument's sake, and see if it means what it is made to mean.

There are some mistakes current which ought to be corrected.

It is an error, quite common, and, among the apologists for slavery, I may venture to say, *universal*, that *all the descendants* of Ham were cursed. The drift of this general belief is thus expressed: "It must be evident to every candid mind, that, in this brief prophetic annunciation of what should follow to his posterity, a condition of servitude is laid upon the children of Ham, especially upon Canaan, and that Shem and Japheth should have the benefit of their service." This is *not* evident. The only evidence in the case is the record; and the following words are a copy of the record: "And Ham, the father of Canaan, saw the nakedness of his father, and told his two brethren without. * * * * And Noah awoke from his wine, and knew what his younger son had done unto him, and he said, Cursed be Canaan; a servant of servants shall he be unto his brethren." Ham was not Noah's younger son. Ham's name is not mentioned in the curse. In four recitals of the names of the sons of Noah the order in which they are named is Shem, Ham, and Japheth. In one place their names are given in the reversed order,— Japheth, Ham, and Shem. The inference is, that Ham was neither the oldest nor the youngest. Ham had four sons— Cush, Misraim, Phut, Canaan. Only one of these names is mentioned in the curse. Noah awoke from his wine, and knew what his *younger* son had done unto him; and he said, Cursed be Canaan. We have seen that Ham was not the younger. We infer from the catalogue of Ham's sons, and from the mention of Canaan's name in the curse, that Canaan was the *younger* son to whom Noah refers. As Canaan's name is singled out, and as he is doubtless the youngest of Ham's children, being mentioned last; and as neither Cush, nor Misraim, nor Phut is mentioned in connection with the misconduct of Ham, nor in connection with the curse of Canaan; and as even Ham himself is not mentioned in the curse—it is impossible to conceive that Noah's curse was intended to rest on *all Ham's posterity.* Canaan was the guilty one whom the patriarch selected as the object of his disfavor. The probability is, that he first saw his grandfather in a fit of drunkenness, and told his father; or, that his father first saw it, and told him; and he, an impudent, irreverent fellow, made sport of his venerable grandfather, who imprudently had taken too much wine. And when Noah became sober again, and was informed how shamelessly this younger member of the family had acted, he said, *cursed be * * * who?* Ham and his descendants? To the *record* for an answer. *Cursed be,*—not Ham, nor Cush, nor Phut,—but CANAAN. There it is. There it will remain. Shame on the ignorance, or the willful perversion of the plain word of God! What a violence and wresting, thus to make Noah's curse pronounced upon Canaan, even on the supposition that he was moved by the Holy Ghost, to include Ham and all his sons and all their posterity; and thence to infer that slavery is their doom, and that, therefore, we can religiously enslave them; and therefore, also, those who are opposed to slavery are infidels and are fighting against God!

The right conclusion as to this curse on Canaan is, if it be a divine warrant for slavery, slavery must be limited to the descendants of Canaan, on whom, by name, and on whom *alone,* the curse was pronounced.

Again: upon the assumption that the curse of Canaan was the utterance of Noah when moved by the Holy Ghost, it is not a valid scriptural justification of slavery, even though it be conceded that the curse was pronounced upon Ham and all his sons and all their posterity.

The advocates of the divine institution of slavery fail, or designedly omit to notice that these words are, at most, only *prophetic.* There is no intimation that they were intended to be understood as ordaining a certain system of labor. If it could be proved or fairly inferred that God in these words ordained slavery, then slavery might be fairly styled a divine institution. But there is no evidence on this. We can regard them in no other light than as a *prophecy*. There is a vast difference between a divine institution and a divine prophecy. The family and the state are the institutions of God, designed for the social and temporal interests of man. The Church is also a divine institution. No man can, without guilt, ignore these. An institution of God has something to do with a man's conscience. Can the same be said of a prophecy? A prophecy may lie hid for ages in the pages of the Bible. Man may be the unconscious instrument of turning the prophecy into history, and neither blame nor merit accrue to him. Not so as to his relations to an institution. An institution implies and enjoins duties. Therefore, if these words of Noah are the constituting formula by which slavery is enjoined as an institution, every one is bound to put himself into some relation to slavery. Every son and daughter of Japheth, and those of Shem, have a right and is bound to have or to try to have at least one slave. Also, every Christian free negro is bound in conscience to put himself into a condition of bondage.

But if the words concerning Canaan lay the foundation of an *institution*, and are a *warrant* for enslaving the children of Ham, by the same rule of interpretation the words concerning Japheth are a *divine warrant* and injunction for his descendants to take possession of the dwellings of Shem. Therefore Europeans, if the pro-slavery theologians are hermeneutically correct as to the curse of Canaan, are permitted and *enjoined* to oust the Shemites from their homes and their thrones. Will any one go so far as to say the *prophecy* as to Japheth is an *institution?* If it is *only a prophecy,* then what are Noah's utterances as to Canaan more than a prophecy also? If one is an instituting formula, so is the other. If one is only a prophecy, so is the other.

But, again: even though this curse was divine, and though it was the ordination of slavery, does it follow that it was intended to continue to the end of time? How do we know but that it was intended only as a temporary arrangement to last only until the death of Japheth and Shem? And also, if God reversed the blessing pronounced on Ham (Gen. ix., 1), why might he not reverse the curse if he saw fit? Indeed, if we are to believe some of the writers, the blessing now rests upon the African in the Southern States, and the curse rests upon the operatives, the *mud-sills*, of the North. The saddle is on the wrong horse.

Here we pause in the examination of the several matters we have proposed to investigate.

Let us not rise from our studies at this time without carrying with us three reflections:

1. The best refutation of error is a correct reading of the Word of God.

2. Let us learn, from the fall of Noah, that no one is safe who goes into temptation.

3. Let us learn, from the misconduct of Ham and Canaan, to honor all rightful authority, even when we cannot approve the words and acts, nor respect the persons of those in authority.

LECTURE II.

––––––•••––––––

ACTS XVII. 26.—"God hath made of one blood all nations of men for to dwell on all the face of the earth."

THERE is an error, quite general, as to the localities where the sons and descendants of Ham settled, and also as to their color. It seems to be commonly believed that all the Hamites settled in Africa, and that they are all negroes. Many suppose they are all under a curse of slavery. Hence, they infer that, by divine appointment, white people have a right to enslave the blacks. Some go so far as to say that all negroes ought to be slaves, and even argue that slavery is the best possible condition for them. It is taken for granted that a black face and crisped hair, or the smallest degree of mixture of Negro blood, is God's warrant and man's authority for enslaving the African.

One of the effects of this general mistake as to the settlement of Ham's sons, and as to the color of his descendants, is to perpetuate the enslaving of the Negro and to continue an unwarranted prejudice against the entire race.

Let us place the matter fairly before us. The question is as to the localities where the sons of Ham settled, and as to the color of his descendants; and especially we are to ascertain, if possible, if the color of a large portion of the human family is connected with Noah's curse on Canaan.

The error is, that all descended from Ham are negroes. We first inquire: What does the Bible say as to the origin and reason of the various colors and peculiarities of the several

2

varieties of the human family? The answer is brief, emphatic, and final,—*not one word.* Not even a hint do we find in the Word of God as to the cause of the various shades of color in the human family. It is an interesting question, and science has busied itself with its solution. With what satisfactoriness, as to results, let the advocates of the different theories say. Let us keep to our present question: What does the *Bible* say about the color of the various races of man? We answer: the Bible says very little about their color, and absolutely nothing as to the time when, or the reasons why, these varieties were introduced. There are a few passages of Scripture in which *black* is descriptive of the person or the dress. Job xxx. 30—"My skin is black upon me." The comment on this, by Barnes, is: "By the mere force of his disease, his skin had become dark and swarthy, though he had not been exposed to the burning rays of the sun." Lamentation iv. 8—"Their visage is blacker than a coal." Patrick, on this, says: "The famine has spoiled their complexion." Lamentation v. 10—"Our skin was black like an oven." Jeremiah adds, as the reason, "because of the terrible famine." Jeremiah viii. 21—"For the hurt of the daughter of my people * * * I am black." On this, Pool paraphrases thus: "I am as those that are clad in deep mourning," and refers to xiv. 2, where we read, "The gates are black unto the ground." Canticles i. 5—"I am black but comely," which Patrick thus explains, "I am as a shepherdess when tanned by lying much abroad in the field." All these refer, you see, to something special. We do read, however, that in the time of Jeremiah (xiii. 23) there were people called Ethiopians, who certainly had some peculiarity as to the color of their skin. He says: "Can the Ethiopian change his skin?" This is an allusion, doubtless, not to a color caused by disease or grief or famine, nor to dress expressive of mourning, but to a people whose color was peculiar, fixed, and well known. We know from parallel sources of information that the Ethiopians were negroes. Jeremiah informs us indirectly that the Ethiopians were negroes. The Ethiopians were descendants from Cush. The word is not Ethiopian in the Hebrew; it is *Cushite.* The Seventy, translating from the Hebrew to the Greek, say *Ethio-*

pian, knowing, as they must have known positively, that the Ethiopians were descended from Cush. The German translation of Luther has Negroland for Ethiopia, *i. e.*, the country of the blacks. We must not fall into mistake or confusion here. Cush, the son of Ham, did not settle in Africa, but in Shinar in Asia. In process of time, as Eusebius, the historian, informs us, a colony of Asiatic Cushites settled in that part of Africa which has since been called Ethiopia proper. Josephus asserts, that "these Ethiopians were descendants of Cush, and that in his time they were still called Cushites by themselves and by all the inhabitants of Asia." "According to Bruce, who traveled in Africa, the Abyssinians have among them a tradition, handed down from time immemorial, that Cush was their father." "Homer divides the Ethiopians into two parts, and Strabo, the geographer, maintains that the division line to which he alluded was the Red Sea." The Cushites of Asia emigrated in part to the west of the Red Sea; so Eusebius also thinks. These, remaining unmixed with other races, have engrossed the general name of Cushite or Ethiopians, while the Asiatic Cushites have become largely mingled with other nations, and are nearly or quite absorbed, or, as a distinct people, well nigh extinct.

Hence, from the allusion of Jeremiah to the skin of the Ethiopian, confirmed and explained by such authorities as Homer, and Strabo, and Herodotus, and Josephus, and Eusebius, we conclude that the Ethiopians were an African branch of the Cushites, who settled first in Asia; and, we conclude also, that these Cushites were negroes. I do not recollect that any information is given us, in any other place in Scripture, as to the color of the descendants of Ham. But is this sufficient, as premises, from which to infer that all Ham's posterity are negroes? The inference rather is, that of all Ham's descendants, the Cushites alone are black, because these are singled out by the prophet to illustrate his doctrine of the impossibility of the human heart to turn from its wickedness. If the descendants of Misraim and of Canaan were of the same color as the Cushite, it is marvelous that Jeremiah should pass them by and introduce an Ethiopian. Misraim, *i. e.*, Egypt, was nearer than

Ethiopia. The Canaanites were upon their borders. Why, then, speak of those at a distance, as an illustration, when others of the same color were nearer—*i. e.*, if Misraim and Canaan, descendants of Ham, were also of the same color with the distant Cushite? But, the learned may say, there were Ethiopian slaves in Jerusalem when Jeremiah wrote, and he therefore naturally introduces them for his purpose of illustration. Granted ;—for it is probable the Cushites were liable to be enslaved at that day, and some authorities assert there were Cushite slaves in Jerusalem at that time. But, if the Canaanites also were black, still, we can not imagine why he should say, " Can the *Cushite* change his skin ?" for if Cushites and Canaanites were alike black, and if there were Canaanite slaves in Jerusalem at the time (and there certainly were), then the prophet, so it seems to us, would phrase his question thus : " Can a *slave* change his skin ?" For what the prophet wanted was an *illustration*. He wanted to introduce a black skin as a permanent, well known variety of the human family. He does not introduce Misraim, or Phut, or Canaan, each of whom was nearer than Cush ; he does not say slave ; he does express his idea by speaking of Cush. Hence Cush alone, of all the descendants of Ham, was black.

There is reason to believe that Cush was the progenitor of the Negro variety of the human family, and that none other of Ham's posterity had these peculiarities. The present inhabitants of the countries where Misraim, Phut, and Canaan settled, certainly have not those peculiarities. The Greeks called the Cushites Ethiopians, and they applied that appellation to no other of Ham's posterity. By Ethiopians the Greeks meant, not *locality* so much as *peculiarity*—the word Ethiopian (in the Greek) meaning *burnt face*.

We have seen that the Ethiopians were black, and that they were the descendants of Cush. There is no evidence, except some disputed assertions respecting the Egyptians, that any other branch of Ham's posterity were of this complexion. None of the races or nations mentioned in Scripture are known to have been negroes but the Cushites.

Therefore, it cannot be proved that all the posterity of Ham were of that complexion. It has never been proved that the Canaanites were black. Besides, it is supposed that the Canaanites are extinct. They no longer exist as a separate people, distinct as to their genealogy. Hence, it would follow that, even if there had been an inspired curse upon them, and if they had been as really negroes as the Cushites, the mere fact that there are certain persons now existing whose skin is black and whose hair is crisped neither proves that they are the descendants of him on whom Noah's curse fell, nor is it in itself a presumption of right on the part of the descendants of Japheth to enslave them.

Is it not wonderful that such a mistake as to the color of Ham's posterity, so difficult to account for and so easily refuted, should have gained so large a belief? Possibly a majority of those whom I address have to this day believed that Noah's curse was by the Lord's authority; and that it rested upon Ham and all his children; and that this curse of bondage was designed to continue to the end of time; and that all the family of Ham were struck black; and that that color is the Lord's mark by which all the world may know who may be subjected to servitude.

It is impossible to meliorate the condition of these downtrodden people while such gross mistakes and such bitter prejudices exist respecting them. It is to correct some of these errors, and to remove, if possible, at least, in some measure, this prejudice, that I have undertaken to expound the curse of Canaan, and to speak on topics kindred to it.

We are speaking of color as a variety in the human family. We have found in the Bible that the Cushite alone was black, and that neither of the other three sons of Ham was of this complexion. We have not a word as to the time when, or the reason why, or the causes by which, this variety was introduced. Let us look at some of the theories on this general question of color.

The mark which the Lord set upon Cain,—what was it? Was it a change of color by which he might be known? The Lord set a mark upon Cain because he had killed his brother. If it was a change of color, the mark would certainly be visible. We can easily suppose that this color could be perpetuated, and thus a new variety, a new race, could have been introduced. But it was not necessary that a *visible* mark should be put upon him in order that Cain should everywhere be known as the murderer. Let a man in any community kill a person; and do you suppose it would be necessary to label him *murderer?* Every one would point at him as he passed; and children, ceasing from their play, would whisper to each other, There goes the murderer. His act would stick to him as indelibly as a change of color. It is not necessary to suppose that any visible mark was set upon Cain. Besides, to assert that he was changed in the manner supposed, and that he thus became the progenitor of those who have borne these peculiarities, will not relieve us of the difficulty. For if Cain was the progenitor of Noah, and if Cain's new peculiarities were perpetuated, then, as Noah was the father of the world's new population, the question would be, not how can we account for any of the human family being black, but how can we account for any being white?

All this speculation as to the change of Cain's color, as a theory for accounting for the variety peculiar to Cush, falls to the ground when we trace back the genealogy of Noah and find that he is descended, not from Cain, but from Seth. Of course, Cain's descendants, no matter what their color, became extinct at the time of the flood.

Calmet introduces a tradition, in his dictionary, as existing among Eastern writers, "that Noah having cursed Ham and Canaan, the effect of his curse was, that not only their posterity were made subject to their brethren, and born, as we may say, in slavery, but that likewise, all on a sudden, the color of their skin became black; for they maintain that all the blacks descended from Ham and Canaan." [Stackhouse, p. 96, note.] To show at what straws a desperate cause will clutch, I have to inform you that this tradition is introduced into a grave argument in defence of slavery by one of its ablest advocates. But please take notice, 1st, this is only a *tradition;* 2d, it assumes that the curse was pronounced on Ham and all his children, which was not the case, if we take the

Bible as a competent witness ; 3d, it declares that Canaan was black, which has never been proved. We dismiss this traditionary and visionary theory as unworthy a grave discussion.

Passing from speculation and tradition, let us approach to theories more tangible. There are only two ways of accounting for the color and hair of the Cushites. These are, either that the Cushites were a native, original variety, produced without natural causes, by the will and direct act of the Creator ; or, that their peculiarities were the effect of climate and circumstances, and have become fixed and permanent by time and continued intermarriage of like with like. It is easy to resolve the remarkable differences observable in the races of the human family into the will and power of the Creator. It might please some if it could be made evident that the Cushite was constitutionally different from all the rest of the human family ; for, in that case, not being of the same blood, there would be less trouble, from conscience, in enslaving them. But the word of God, by his servant Paul (Acts xvii. 26), will stand to the end of time. "God hath made of one blood all nations of men for to dwell on all the face of the earth." The Cushites are not constitutionally different from the rest of the human family. "We contemplate (says Prichard, 545), among all the diversified tribes who are endued with reason and speech, the same internal feelings, appetencies, aversions, the same inward convictions, the same sentiments of subjection to invisible powers, and, more or less fully developed, of accountableness or responsibility to unseen avengers of wrong and agents of retributive justice, from whose tribunal men cannot, even by death, escape. We find everywhere the same susceptibility (though not always in the same degree of forwardness or ripeness) of improvement, of admitting the cultivation of those universal endowments, of opening the eyes to the more clear and luminous views which Christianity unfolds, of becoming moulded to the institutions of religion and civilized life : in a word, the same inward and mental nature is to be recognized in all the races of men." So that we must insist upon unity, although we see and admit the variety.

It is an ingenious but certainly too fanciful a way of ac-

counting for the varieties of mankind, to say that the three
sons of Noah were types of the three colors into which the
family of man is divided. Their names, given probably by
Moses as historic, and not by Noah as prophetic, certainly
have meanings. These meanings marvelously coincide with
the complexion, and condition, and mission of some of the suc-
cessors of Noah's sons respectively. The colors of the human
family are white, black, and red. Japheth means *fair;*
and the Europeans, Japheth's descendants, are *white.* Ham
means *hot* or *burnt;* and the most multitudinous of Ham's four
lines of progeny, the Cushites, who, although at first settled in
Asia, afterwards migrated to Africa and overspread the entire
Continent, except Egypt and the Barbary States, are *black.*
Canaan means *humiliated;* and the word is an expressive
epitome of their history, for the Canaanites were in part driven
out of their country by the Hebrews, in part utterly extermi-
nated, and in part reduced to slavery. A colony of Canaanites from Tyre founded Carthage, which was finally taken by
the Romans. The Canaanites are thought to be extinct. How
comprehensive the word which designates them—Canaan, *i. e.,*
humiliated! Shem means *name;* and may have been given
to this branch of the family of Noah by Moses, writing by inspiration, because to it God had revealed his name, and out
of it he was to come whose name—JESUS—is above every
name, and the only name given among men whereby they
must be saved. If we receive these names as intended to
be significant, we are not at liberty to conclude that they were
given by Noah,—intended by him as prophetic of what the
color and condition of these sons were to be for all time to
come. As prophetic, if dated in Noah's day, the prophecy has
failed, for Shem became servant to Ham; Canaan was at one
time mighty; the descendants of Ham did not all settle in a
hot country, and were not black, except one line of them. It
is not probable that Shem, Ham, Japheth, Canaan, were the
names they received when children, but the comprehensive
and significant historic names which Moses gave them. We
must remember that Moses wrote these histories. We must
remember that by this time, when the Hebrews were in the

wilderness, and when Moses was compiling their history and giving them the moral precepts and the civil code, Europe, Asia, and Africa were populously settled. We may easily suppose that, in sketching a summary of the genealogy and settlement of the nations in the three great divisions of the earth, some one *comprehensive* word would be used, if possible, *characteristic* of the whole. We do the same thing. We say John Bull, and Brother Jonathan, and the Sick Man, &c., meaning Great Britain, and the United States, and Turkey. At the time when Moses wrote, the Europeans must have been known as the *fair* or the *white* people. And so it was descriptive and comprehensive to speak of them and their ancestor under the one suggestive word, Japheth. By this time the Cushites were largely spread over Africa, and, as the Cushites were black, all the family of which they were the most numerous would naturally be called the burnt-faces, or the *black*, or Ham. And as the Hebrews were of that family to which God revealed his name, and out of which the great new Name was to come, it was natural to call themselves and their ancestor Shem. As the Canaanites were at this time greatly deteriorated in morals from the standard and example of Melchizedek and Abimelech, and as Moses knew by inspiration that the Hebrews were soon to take possession of their land, he characterizes them and their ancestor as Canaan, *i. e.*, the *humiliated*. The probability therefore is, that these names, so full of meaning and so descriptive of the people to whom they are given, are to be considered as originating with Moses, and not as the names by which the children of Noah were known in their own day. The names are certainly historically significant, but can hardly be received as having been given in their childhood, and prophetic of what these several branches were destined to be.

We have been considering the first of the two theories which can be admitted to account for the peculiarities of the Cushite. We find but little to favor the idea of an *original*, distinct variety, from the consideration of the names of Noah's sons. Let us ever adhere to the excellent rule never to account for anything *by miracle*, which can be accounted for by natural causes and the forces of nature. We honor God when we honor his laws. We recognize his presence and power when we trace and admire the regular operations of the forces of nature, as well as when we see and admit undoubted miracles. We admit that the Creator could have miraculously turned Cain into a negro as a mark by which he might be known. We admit that these peculiarities might have been perpetuated, and thus a variety introduced at an early stage of the history of man. We admit that Canaan might have been struck black for his guilty complicity in dishonoring Noah, and might have been the progenitor of a new variety in the human family. But to these admitted possibilities we object, 1st, that not a hint is anywhere to be found in the Bible that God introduced this variety for any of the foregoing reasons, or in any of the foregoing ways. We object, 2d, that Canaan's posterity were not black, and the Cushites were. We object, 3d, that in no instance can it be shown that a miracle has occurred when the ordinary operation of the laws of nature is adequate to produce the result of which we seek the solution. A sudden change of skin so as to become permanent and perpetuated would be a miracle. But if a change of color and hair has occurred, and has, in the course of time, become a fixed variety in the human family, then it was not miraculous; and, of course, it was not intended to be a *stigma ;* but it has occurred according to laws and forces of nature.

Let us not, then, introduce either the theory of an original variety, or of a miraculous change, until we inquire if any facts can be found to show that the variety may have been introduced by slow processes of forces which have always been in operation. Let us look at facts which the observation of the thoughtful has spread before us. Consider what effects differences of organic structure, differences of temperament, differences of propensity, difference of habit, difference of domestic influences, the difference of food and air and exercise and climate,—consider what effects such forces are capable of producing in the case of those born of the same family. These are facts, and these are forces which, while they do not divest the differences of color in the human family of mystery and difficulty, afford suggestions as to how these, now permanent, varieties may have originated.

For the effect of climate upon color, there are interesting and instructive facts as to the Jews in India and in Northern Europe. There are, as we all know, fixed and unalterable features in the Jew. You recognize a Jew at once, whatever his complexion, language, or nativity, by his physiognomy. Climate has not changed his features, but has had an effect upon his color and hair. In Poland and Germany he has a fair complexion and light hair. "The scorching sun of India has curled and crisped his hair and blackened his skin, so that his features alone distinguish him from the native Hindoo." On the Malabar coast are two colonies of Jews—the old and the new colony—separated by color, and known as the Black Jews and the White Jews. The old colony are the Black Jews, and have been longer subjected to the influence of the climate.

The use we have a right to make of this fact, as to a change of color and hair in a colony of Jews, is, to infer that it is not necessary to suppose an original variety with the characteristics of the Negro ; nor to suppose a miraculous change as a stigma in the case of Cain, or Ham, or Canaan. If climate has effected so marked a change in this colony of Shemites, how can we deny that it may have produced similar changes in that branch of the Hamites which peopled the torrid regions of Africa?

If the facts and the discussion now submitted shall correct errors into which any of you may have fallen, and if they shall aid, even in a small degree, in removing prejudices against a portion of the family of man—our own flesh and blood, as our common Creator expressly declares—I shall not have labored in vain to bring the truth before you. Whether or not the origin and cause of certain peculiarities in the Ethiopian can be accounted for, it may be confidently asserted that the color of the Cushite is no way, scripturally, historically, or ethnologically, connected with the curse of Canaan. It is not a mark of the doom to servitude of all the children of Ham ; it is not a warrant for enslaving them; it is not a justifiable reason for entertaining prejudices against them.

If what has now been said has corrected any of your mistakes, let it also be the means of removing any prejudices of which any of you may be conscious. The Cushites are in an humbled condition all over the earth. They are under the heel of the white man in our country. Can their condition be meliorated while they are at the double disadvantage of slavery and prejudice? Prejudice is bitter and supercilious. Slavery is heavy. Slavery says to the Negro, Get down before me, for I am more powerful than you. Prejudice says to the Negro, Stand aside, for I am better than you. It is not easy to say whether slavery or prejudice is the greater hindrance to the melioration of the condition of the colored people of this country. There is much denunciation of the South because there the black man is enslaved. Let these fierce denunciators ask themselves if they are more the friend of the Negro than the slaveholder, if they are conscious of these prejudices. No man can consistently decry slavery, while in his soul he loathes the black man only because of his color. First cast out the beam out of thine own eye, and then shalt thou see clearly to cast out the mote out of thy brother's eye. Charity begins at home. To put the case in a strong and striking light: Supposing all the sons of Ham are negroes; supposing all the negroes are under the curse of bondage and servitude; supposing they are to remain so until in the Millenium they shall stretch forth their unshackled hands unto God; supposing they are inferior and deficient (as their father Ham certainly was deficient, to wit, in strong principles of respect and duty to his father);—and we, being as we are, proud, honored, and thankful to be the descendants of Japheth (intellectual, enterprising, conquering Japheth),—what shall we do? We may do either of these two things—we may, as Ham and Canaan did, expose the degradation of the weak and fallen, and magnify it, and hold it up to scorn; or, we may do as our honorable father Japheth did, turn away our eyes in grief for the dishonor of the fallen; and, instead of delighting and making gain out of the disgrace of our own flesh and blood, we may cover the despised Negro and the slave with the mantle of sorrow for his condition, and of concealment of his shame, and of hope and effort for his restoration. Wherein are those better than Ham and Canaan who expose to contempt the fall of the weak and the degradation of the inferior? Boasting that we are born to a better condition, let us imitate the noble and dutiful deportment of our father, Japheth, by doing what we can to protect and befriend those who are unable to help themselves, until they shall, in God's good time and wise providence, take their places among men, equal as of a common origin, equal as involved in the ruins of Adam's fall, equal as endowed by their Maker with the inalienable right to life, liberty, and the pursuit of happiness, equal as the welcome beneficiaries of the same grace of salvation, equal as amenable to the same tribunal of judgment, equal as candidates for an endless existence of blessedness or despair.

God hath made of one blood all nations. Let this declaration teach us charity and compassion towards all mankind; let it teach us our dependence on God; let it teach us, while we prize and rejoice in existence, to prize and rejoice in that divine Saviour who has come to repair the ruins of the fall, and to secure for the insolvent a full remission, and, for those who have no inheritance, a share in his honors and in his unspeakable riches.

LECTURE III.

THE FUTURE OF THE CUSHITE.

———◆◆◆———

PSALM LXVIII. 31.—Ethiopia shall soon stretch out her hands unto God.

GENESIS IX. 24, 25.—And Noah awoke from his wine, * * * and he said, Cursed be Canaan.

PSALM LXVIII. 31.—Ethiopia shall soon stretch out her hands unto God.

PSALM LXXII. 12.—He shall deliver * * * the poor also, and him that hath no helper.

PSALM LXXXVII. 4.—Behold * * * Ethiopia; this man was born there.

ISAIAH LVIII. 6.—Is not this the fast that I have chosen, * * * to let the oppressed go free, and that ye break every yoke?

JEREMIAH XXXIV. 17.—Therefore, thus saith the Lord; ye have not hearkened unto me, in proclaiming liberty, every one to his brother, and every man to his neighbor: behold, I proclaim a liberty for you, saith the Lord, to the sword, to the pestilence, and to the famine.

It is unnecessary, for our present purpose, to enter into an exact exposition of these passages of sacred Scripture. Their tenor is all we care for. This it is not easy for the candid to mistake. These texts have a bearing upon the matter in hand, to wit, the *probable future* of the Cushites or Ethiopians, or, as they are usually styled, *the Negroes.*

The words of Noah, wrested to include the entire posterity of Ham, and interpreted by those whose social, or pecuniary, or political interests are involved, are held up as the inspired word of Jehovah, dooming the Cushite to perpetual bondage.

The words quoted from David, Isaiah, and Jeremiah, lead us to expect that, under the influence of the Gospel, in the times when it shall have free course, slavery will come to an end, and the Ethiopian, *i. e.*, the Negro race, will be liberated, enlightened, and evangelized.

There is, certainly, a discrepancy here. One or the other of these inferences, as to the future of this large part of the

3

human race, must be wrong. They cannot each be right. The word of God cannot contradict itself. It is only by violence and ingenious interpretation, and by ignoring or perverting history, that the perpetual servitude of the African can be derived from the words of Noah ; whereas, the natural meaning and agreeing tenor of the words of David, Isaiah, and Jeremiah, is, that the Ethiopian shall be delivered from oppression and the yoke. It is worth noticing, too, in deciding which of these opposing meanings to accept, that, as to Noah's utterance, there is no solemn preface—" thus saith the Lord ;" whereas, in all the passages quoted from the other sacred penmen, there is either a direct address to God or from God, under authority and inspiration. This is a noticeable difference, and a very conclusive argument in the question as to which of these opposing declarations, in reference to the posterity of Ham, we are to accept as the mind of God. If Noah and the *pro-slavery* school are right, then David, Isaiah, and Jeremiah, and the *anti-slavery* school, are wrong. But the presumption is that Noah and company are wrong, for Noah spake as he was moved by wine and chagrin ; and the company which indorse his curse on Canaan speak as they are moved by their social, or pecuniary, or political interests. On the other hand, David, and Isaiah, and Jeremiah indicate, both by their prefaces and in their utterances, that they are but the mouth of the Lord ; and as to Isaiah and Jeremiah, their temporal interests were jeoparded by their declarations ; while Noah might safely count on having the majority and the favor of his family, when he decided, with patriarchal authority, that Canaan should serve his brethren.

We conclude, therefore, that it is the will and prophecy of · God that the oppressed shall go free, and the yoke of slavery shall be broken.

Here we might rest, awaiting in calm expectation the working out, by the machinery of Providence, the eternal purposes of the Almighty. But, while we stand still and see the salvation of God, we may look into the progress of his movements, and may study the nature of those noiseless but mighty forces by which he works.

It is clear that the Ethiopian is included in the gospel pro-gramme. Ethiopia shall stretch out her hands unto God. Ethiopia is Cush. Cush is the generic name for the descendants of the oldest son of Ham. The Cushites, or Ethiopians, are the Negroes. The tenor of the several passages of the Bible quoted is, that slavery will come to an end under the gospel dispensation, and that the black man will be liberated, enlightened, and evangelized.

Dr. Thornwell concedes this much. He says, "That the design of Christianity is to secure the perfection of the race, is obvious from all its arrangements; and that, when this end shall have been consummated, slavery must cease to exist, is equally clear." He, however, makes a condition of bondage the means of perfecting the African ; whereas, we shall show that slavery is a great hindrance to his perfection.

It need not be argued before a Christian audience that the whole earth is to be filled with the knowledge of the Lord; that Christ is a light to lighten the Gentiles ; that the pagans will cast away their idols and renounce their errors ; that when Jesus, as the crucified atoning Savior, shall have been lifted up to the attention of all the world, he will attract the faith of all classes and conditions of mankind. One of the prophecies quoted (Ps. 87, 4) reads thus—"I will make mention of Rahab and Babylon to them that know me : behold Philistia, and Tyre, with Ethiopia ; this man was born there." Upon which ALEXANDER remarks, " The nations thus announced as belonging to God's people are mere samples of the whole Gentile world. * * * Rahab is an enigmatical name, given to Egypt by the Prophet Isaiah. * * * The conversion of Cush, or Ethiopia, had already been foretold by David. * * * Babylon is named instead of Assyria. * * * The idea of regeneration, or spiritual birth, applied in the New Testament to individuals, is here applied to nations, who are represented as born again."

It becomes a question for candid, thoughtful, Christian philanthropists—*Can the gospel have free course and be glorified among those in a condition of servitude, such as slavery is in some of these States?* Can a slave receive that development, and

maturity, and symmetry of character, of which, as a human
being, he is susceptible under the influences of the truth and
spirit of God? If he can, then a condition of slavery is compatible with the highest development and culture of man, and
may continue as a condition of human society under the
splendors of earth's millenial glory. If he cannot, then let
it be said that he cannot; and let us, by maintaining the truth
in this matter, do what we can to prevent the extension of a
system of labor which is not compatible with the free and full
play of the gospel in effecting the highest culture of beings
made, like ourselves, in the likeness and image of God.

To prevent misapprehension, and to simplify the question,
we must remember that this is not to us, from the stand-point
we occupy in this house and on the Lord's day, a question of
political economy: and, therefore, it is not pertinent to our
object to compare the net profits or the physical comforts of
laborers under the two systems—slave and free. Nor is it a
question, as we feel warranted and bound to discuss it, of party
policy: and, therefore, it is not pertinent to the place, nor to
my purpose, to say anything as to immediate emancipation as
a war measure. What I wish to say would have been, in the
main, as appropriately said fifty or five hundred years ago;
and, if true, will be so when you and I shall have ceased to
act our appointed parts in the grand drama of history.

What I wish to hold forth is, that the gospel of the grace
of God is an *educational force*,—developing, elevating, purify-
ing, maturing those who are the subjects of it,—in a word,
not only saving, but perfecting men. And I propose, also, to
show that a system of labor in which there is not a felt freedom to make a contract as to the kind, and amount, and pay
of services rendered, with an admitted right to go and come
at pleasure, and to be the head of one's family, and to trade,
and to do such things as freemen can do, is *a hindrance to the
full educative force of the gospel.*

The half of the truth may be equal to a downright misrepresentation. It is a misrepresentation of the purpose and
power of the truth as it is in Jesus, to hold that it is only a

refuge for a sinful and condemned soul. It is that, and that is much. But that is not all. That view, alone, is certainly narrow. To accept the salvation procured and offered by Christ *only* because he saves from hell, is, at least, to render the recipient liable to the suspicion of selfishness. We would be apt to think that if there were credible testimony presented to such a Christian of there being no hereafter or no hell, he would fall back from his profession and follow Christ no more. We think Christ is a portion as well as a refuge. He is our strength, and light, and life. Christ in the soul is as much a force as leaven and salt in their appropriate spheres of operation. Christ's instruction is, that *all the capabilities of human nature must co-operate with this heavenly power.* Work out your own salvation ; grow in grace and knowledge,—your bodies, temples of the Holy Ghost. I pray God, says Paul, that your whole spirit, and soul, and body be preserved blameless unto the coming of our Lord Jesus Christ. Now, to say that the gospel can save men in a state of bondage as *really* as it can save men in a condition of freedom, none will deny. But to say that the gospel can save men as *fully*, and develop them as *symmetrically*, and mature them as *perfectly*, in a state of bondage, like that in the Southern States, as in a state of Freedom, we unhesitatingly deny. The foot of a China lady is as *really* a *human* foot as the foot of a miner or of a hod-carrier ; but the small shoe prevents its growth. It is a *live* foot, of course ; but it is neither large enough for a foundation, nor strong enough for support. Circumstances have not killed it, but have hindered its growth. The unnatural usages of society have not intercepted the connection between that foot and that lady's heart; there is a flow and a circulation of the vital influences, but there is a hindrance to that full expansion and growth which are the normal results of the unhindered flow and circulation of the vital force. What the small, tight, cramping shoe is to the foot, slavery is to the human soul. It does not prevent his becoming and being a renewed man in Christ Jesus; but it is a hindrance to the full development of his capabilities as an intellectual, moral, and immortal being. It does not, and cannot, cut off the connection between the Christian slave and Christ his Head, but it interferes with the culture of some of those powers by which men, as men, and Christians, as Christian men, come into contact with men and things. "A human being is a member of the community, not as a limb is a member of the body, or as a wheel is a member of a machine, intended only to contribute to some general, joint result. He was created, not to be merged in the whole, as a drop in the ocean, or as a particle of sand on the sea-shore, and to aid only in composing a mass; he is an ultimate being, made for his own perfection as the highest end [next to the glory of God],—made to sustain an individual existence, and to serve others only so far as consists with his own virtue and progress."* There is much talk about the progress of society. The progress of society is conditioned, and measured, by the aggregate advance of the individuals who constitute the community, state, or nation. Nothing is so grand, nothing is so much in accordance with the object of the mission of Christ, as to give an individual mind a consciousness of its separate worth. "The progress of society consists in bringing out the individual, in giving him a consciousness of his own being, and in quickening him to strengthen and elevate his own mind."* "Free will, God has ordained. With man rests the responsibilities of applying it to the relations of life, as well as to the duties of the soul toward God. Liberty is necessary to the exercise of the will. Woe to the man, or to the Government, or to the institution that puts restraint upon that which God has made free."† You may *regulate* the *actions* of a man in society; but it is tyranny, not government, to put him into circumstances where he cannot think, and weigh evidence, and balance motives, and choose, and speak, and act according to the free will which God has given him, as a divine warrant for individual, and separate, and independent existence. A man or a nation may, indeed, exist without freedom; the slave may be, materially and physically, in a better condition than the citizen; under a pious and prudent patriarch, men would doubtless be happier than under the changing rule of a capricious and unprin-

---

* Channing.　　　　　　　　† De Tocqueville.

cipled democracy; "but such is not the normal condition of creatures endowed with reason and with conscience, and constituted by their Creator heirs of immortality." Law, and order, and trade, and the training of a family, are the legitimate studies of intelligent creatures. Such studies are necessary, in order that the conscience and reason may be rightly trained, fully developed, and properly exercised. Conscience and reason cannot be in a condition of health without proper exercise. But how can this condition of health, and vigor of conscience and of reason in the study of law, and order, and trade, and in the training of a family, be attained, in a condition of servitude,—a condition in which man, thus highly endowed, is under the restraint of an authority, in the acceptance and modification of which his free will, and reason, and conscience are utterly ignored? A man is a man only as he is educated. Education is not strictly confined to what is learned in school or from books. It consists in the worth of the things learned, in the mental training received, and in the skill to properly use the knowledge and power thus acquired. If God has given me a hand, he impliedly imposes the obligation of its right use. I cannot, without fault, let it wither at my side; and you cannot, without blame, tie my hand and paralyze its powers. The mental powers which God has given me are God's command to me to do what I can in developing and applying them for my own and for others' benefit. You fight against God, you invade his prerogative, when you put me in circumstances restraining the rightful use of these mental capabilities. The Creator impliedly grants me the privilege and imposes upon me the obligation of training my intellectual and moral faculties (my conscience, my reason, my free will, my affections) in the mere fact that he has endowed me with such capabilities. Woe to him that stands in the way of the development of these endowments! Woe to that system of labor or of government, whether on a small scale or on a large scale, whether in the shops of the North or the fields of the South, whether in the family or in the State, which puts an inelastic band upon the human soul and prevents its growth! Every kind of despotism does this. All work with no respite for recreation or mental culture does this. Many a parent, and many a master mechanic, and many a store-keeper in our boasted free North does this when he exacts too many hours' service, and does not afford opportunities to those under his authority and employment to relax their bodies from toil and their minds from care, and does not aid and encourage his children, his operatives, and his clerks, to improve and store their capacious and immortal minds. Slavery does this. It is in its very nature to do this. And this is my great objection to slavery. It is, viewed from this stand-point, in its aspects and bearings upon the development of the individual that the chief objection lies. It is not that the slave is not kindly treated; not that he does not get an equivalent for his work; not that he is worse conditioned as to physical comfort,—that I object to this system of labor. It is because the system does not and cannot, in its very nature, recognize a slave as a man in the just sense of the word.

Let us not lose sight of our point. I make but one in my argument. I say nothing about stealing the man, robbing him of his labor, rupturing the ties of nature in separating him, by sale, from those who are dear to him. I only say that enslaving him hinders his symmetrical growth and full development as a being endowed with intellectual and moral capabilities. Slavery interferes with that culture which the gospel, when it has free play, always ensures, and which it is its object to accomplish. "That the design of Christianity is to secure the perfection of the (human) race, is obvious from all its arrangements;"* and that, in order to accomplish this object, slavery must cease, is equally clear. The slaves among the Greeks, says Mitford, "were forbidden everything manly, and were commanded everything humiliating of which man is capable." Says Prichard, speaking of the effect of slavery upon the natives in the regions whence African slaves are exported, "The tribes on the coast have been reduced to the lowest state of physical and moral degradation by the vices and calamities attendant upon the traffic. They are ever on the watch to seize the wives and children of the neighboring clans, and to sell.

* Thornwell.

them to strangers. Many sell their own. Almost every retired corner of the land has been the scene of hateful rapine and slaughter * * perpetrated in cold blood for the love of gain." We need not go to ancient Greece nor to pagan Africa to learn the character and effects of slavery, and to learn how it operates as a hindrance to the culture and development of the slave. Is it a right of humanity to hold property? Is it a right for a man to claim his wife and children as his own? Is it a right of humanity to be protected in life and limbs? Is it a right of humanity for a man, feeling sick, *to say* that he is sick? Let us see how these rights are treated where slavery is the established system of labor. "In South Carolina a slave can acquire no right which does not, the instant that it is transferred to him, pass to his master." "The owner of a female slave may give her to one person and her children to another." In Virginia a man cannot be indicted for beating his own slave. No valid contract can be made with a slave without the consent of his master. In South Carolina it is lawful for any person to seize from a slave the horses he bred, and deliver them to the nearest magistrate. In South Carolina there is a penalty attached to trading with a slave. All the acquisitions of a slave are the property of his master. The master or overseer, and not the slave, is the judge whether the slave is too sick to work. In Alabama a man, by will, gave his slaves their choice to be free or continue the slaves of his daughter. They were held to be her slaves because they had "no capacity to choose." ☞ No capacity to choose!! The *divine right* of *free will* denied them! The status of the African in Georgia, whether bond or free, is such that he has no civil, social, or political rights whatever, except such as are bestowed on him by statute. Slaves cannot contract marriage, nor does their cohabitation confer any legal rights on their children. In most of the slave States it is made a high crime and misdemeanor to teach a slave to read or write, or to give him any book or pamphlet, &c., &c.* Can any man say, after this, that "a slave has all the rights which belong essentially to humanity"?

* New York Evening Post, January 29, 1862.

The foregoing are judicial decisions or legislative enactments in the slave States. Are such laws, or are they not, hindrances to the development and culture of a human soul? No wonder (as Dr. Thornwell, the ablest defender of slavery who ever wielded a pen in its behalf, admits) "the civilized world is unanimous in its execration of slavery." And yet he maintains that "subjection to a master is the state in which the African is most effectually trained to the moral end of his being."

Here we pause to gather up the materials of our arguments, and to state our conclusion. We learn from the Scriptures that the gospel is intended for all the human family. We learn that with all the varieties of colors and conditions, all the races are of one blood. We conclude that the gospel is offered to the Ethiopian as well as to the European—to the slave as well as to the freeman. We learn that it is the design and effect of the truth, as it is in Jesus, to develope and perfect men as individuals, by the cultivation of their mental and moral capabilities. But we find a certain institution, so called, which, in its very nature, is a hindrance to that development and cultivation. Warranted in expecting that every stumbling block will be removed, and every yoke will be broken, so that the gospel may have free course that it may be glorified, we conclude that slavery is not the best condition for the Cushite, and that it will come to an end.

With this conclusion there is nothing in Noah's curse on Canaan which does not coincide. For, even admitting that his curse was inspired and authorized, it is only a *prophecy*, and not an *institution*. As a prophecy, it is enough to say that it was fulfilled when the Gibeonites became and continued slaves to the Hebrews, from the time of the conquest of Canaan until the return of the Jews from their captivity in Babylon. As an inspired prophecy, even, there is nothing in it to warrant the doctrine which some derive from it—that slavery must continue to the end of time. It is enough that it was fulfilled in the service rendered to the Hebrews by the Canaanites.

We come now to the question, What is the destiny of the

people of color in our country? With this question the nation is moved. The earthquake, whose rumblings have been heard for years, has shaken the foundations of our Government. There is not an hour of the day in which millions of men are not thinking and talking about this great upheaval. The whole world is interested in our crisis. State it as you please, you cannot leave the Negro out of the case, as in some way the occasion of these calamities which have come upon us, at which anxious millions at home and abroad hold their breath, awaiting the result. Of course, there are various theories as to the cause of the rebellion, and there is abounding crimination and re-crimination, and there are various projects as to the best way of ending the war, and there are all kinds of prophecies as to the results, in the bearing of this agitation upon slavery and the black man. In all this, can any one close his eyes to the fact that the condition of the Negro, like long-neglected Central Africa, is looming up into notice? This is a great gain to the interests of our common humanity. It is an item of great importance as to the destiny of the Cushites among us, that their *presence and condition must be taken into account by the thinkers and leaders of the pulpit, the press, and the halls of legislation.* Never again can public sentiment go to sleep on this volcano. Slavery, *pro* and *con*, or *con* and *pro*—it is not material which way you state it—slavery is the cause of all our national troubles. It is a fact. Accept it we must. Slavery is the cause, direct or indirect, of all our troubles; and slavery involves the condition of the Negro. In one part of the country he is under the burden of slavery; in another part of the country he is under the equally heavy burden of prejudice. It is pertinent to inquire how the free blacks of the North became the objects of this prejudice, and how it is, with so much heated opposition to slavery here, they continue under this disadvantage. The solution is easy, and can be briefly stated. It is the effect of the slavery which once prevailed at the North, and which still prevails at the South, together with an impression, more or less general, of the mental imbecility of the African, and his fated inferiority to the European. It is not the *color*, alone, but the *condition*, of the black man—at the South enslaved, at the North considered and treated as inferior—which causes this prejudice. This feeling toward him is as effectual a barrier as can be reared against his advance to the high improvement and privileges of which he is capable, and to which the gospel destines and entitles him.

In considering the destiny of the black man in this country, the next item we venture to set down is, that *he will be delivered from bondage and from prejudice.* When or how slavery will come to an end in America, I say not. That is not a question for the pulpit. All that the pulpit can legitimately say is to repeat, with a *thus-saith-the-Lord*, "Ethiopia shall soon stretch out her hands unto God"—He (Christ) shall break every yoke—He shall deliver him that hath no helper. What the necessities and policies and objects of this great civil war may lead to, no man is far-seeing enough to conjecture. But when we consider the near approach of the year 1867, in which, as a year of wonders, so many prophetic periods terminate—when we consider that Africa is being explored to its centre and found to contain so vast a wealth, and so vast facilities for bringing it to the markets of the world, and so vast a population, and that that population is most degraded just where the traffic in slaves is carried on, and that this exploration is occurring just when greater attention is being turned to the condition of the Negro in our country than ever before—when we consider that the tripod on which Slavery has sat, and with magic power fascinated the people of this land, and swayed their thinking and their voting for nearly a century, is tottering, because its legs are loosened (for sugar and tobacco and cotton can be raised by free labor, and elsewhere than at the South), so that the vaticinations of this fury cannot again control the credence she was wont to demand—when we consider that, in the march of events, the law is that of a geometrical progression, or the law of attraction, doubly and still doubly strong as the bodies approach the centre of attracting influence—when we consider the "unanimity of the civilized world in their execration of slavery"—when we consider that every crisis is with violence, and that the sharpest

lightning and the most terrific crash of thunder is often just as
the cloud is about to break, and give us the blue sky and the
sunshine again—when we consider that, notwithstanding the
bitterness of the political discussions of the past four years, and
amid all the clangor of the present strife, revivals of religion at
home, and home efforts to promote Christianity abroad, have
never advanced more successfully—when we consider that the
Cushite, and his condition, South and North (once an almost
forbidden topic in the pulpit, the press, and the parlor) is now
the question which meets us at every turn and is discussed in
every place—when we consider the success of Liberia and
Hayti, and that the Governments of Europe have acknowledged
them as Governments, and that, within the past week, a propo-
sition to acknowledge them was made in our Senate—when all
these things are considered, we may venture to say that, whatever the future may reveal as to slavery and those afflicted by
it—the master, and the Negro, and the loyal freemen of the
North—we shall *never*, NEVER again see these opened questions
of slavery and the slave-power closed by a return to the former
condition of things. The world is moving. We venture to assert that all these noticeable providences are streaks of light
shooting up into the sky—harbingers of the morning which is
about to break. These facts and events help us to answer the
question as to the destiny of the Negro in our country. That destiny, whether remote or near, I feel confident, is, that he will be
delivered from slavery and from prejudice. This destiny will be
wrought out by means, and not by miracle. God does not work
by miracle where means are adequate. The means are adequate
to the end. Time—perhaps a longer time than some of you
imagine or desire—will be necessary to work out these certain
results. One of the means has already been hinted at, to wit:
slave labor will never again be as profitable as formerly.
" Money makes the mare go." When it is not profitable to
keep slaves, probably there will be a great decline in religion.
Our fellow Christians at the South will become as infidel as the
abolitionists, when their religious institutions are found not to
pay. There is now some reason to apprehend a fall from grace,

for there is a fall in the price of a field-hand from twelve
hundred dollars and upwards to less than a thousand; and
slaves in Charleston, once hired at about two hundred dollars a
year, have been hired out for about fifty. It is astonishing how
the price of things affects the religious sentiments. I suspect
that the once slave-holding people of the North were moved as
much by the sordid considerations of pelf as by the high motives
of piety in the emancipation of their slaves. The same
motives may yet rule in South Carolina. It looks very much
as if, ere long, slavery " *won't pay.*"

Another of the means by which the coming changes will
be effected, is the *dissemination of light* as to the Bible argument in behalf of slavery, and as to the history and capabilities of the colored man. The times of this ignorance God has
seemed to wink at. But now there is a spirit of inquiry
awakened. The false and damaging interpretation of the
curse of Canaan will be exposed. The difference between an
institution and a prophecy will be noticed. The exclusion of
Cush from the curse will be insisted upon. The true genealogy of the Negro will be known. The capabilities of the African, for education and government, will be admitted when the
testimony is laid before the candid. The history of what he
has accomplished as a force in the world, and the facts as to
what he is now doing in Sierra Leone, Liberia, and Hayti, will
be studied. These are the means by which the Negro will be
delivered from the oppression which weighs him down,—an
oppression of one kind at the North, and of another kind at
the South. Let me detain you a moment as to this matter of
his *capability.* " Cush is often referred to by the prophets as
a powerful and splendid empire " [Alexander]. The Ethiopian eunuch was prime minister to Candace, the queen. Lok-
man, a black, thick-lipped Ethiopian slave, in the days of
David, wrote fables, yet extant, and is still called, by Mahom-
etans, THE WISE. Benoit, the *holy black*, is highly revered in
the Romish Church. Henry Diaz, extolled in all the histories of Brazil, was a commander of talents, sagacity, and con-
summate experience. Hannibal (not the Carthagenian), an

African negro, of good education, was lieutenant-general and director of artillery under Peter the Great. Don Juan Latino, a negro, was a teacher of the Latin language, at Seville, in Spain. Kislar-Aga, a negro in high position in Constantinople, was a man of "great wisdom and profound knowledge." Anthony William Amo, a native of Guinea, took the degree of doctor of philosophy at the University of Wittemberg, was skilled in the knowledge of the Greek and Latin languages, and gave lectures on philosophy with great acceptance. He was a professor. Job Ben Solomon, from the river Gambia, was a slave in Maryland. He found his way to England, and was received with distinction at the Court of St. James. He translated several Arabic manuscripts. He could repeat the Koran from memory. James Eliza John Capitein was born in Africa. He studied at Leyden, employed himself in painting, and acquired a knowledge of the Latin, Greek, Hebrew, and Chaldaic languages. He published several pieces in Latin and a volume of sermons. Thomas Fuller, a native of Africa, lived near Alexandria, in Virginia. He had a surprising facility for calculation. Being asked how many seconds in seventy years, seven months, and seven days, he answered in a minute and a half. On reckoning it, a person said to him, "You are wrong." "Have you not forgotten the leap-years?" said the negro. This omission was supplied, and the number then agreed with his answer. Ottobah Cugoano was born in Africa. He published a work on slavery and the slave-trade, which discovered a sound and vigorous mind, and was translated into French. Olandad Equiano, an African: his published writings are familiarly known in England. Benjamin Bannaker, a negro, of Maryland, applied himself to astronomy; he published almanacs in Philadelphia. James Derham was once a slave in Philadelphia. When only twenty-one years old he was the most distinguished physician in New Orleans. Dr. Rush says, "I found him very learned. I thought I could give him information concerning the treatment of diseases, but I learned more from him than he could expect from me." Paul Cuffee, whose father was an African and mother an Indian, was known and honored by persons of the first respectability in England and the United States. Few could remain long in his presence without forgetting their prejudice against color and feeling their hearts expand with juster sentiments towards the most injured portion of mankind. We will not extend the catalogue, though I have abundant materials. Blumenbach boldly affirms "there is no savage people who have distinguished themselves by such examples of perfectibility and capacity for scientific cultivation."

Let these facts suffice as a sample, and let the capability of the Negro be admitted. It is assumed that he is not fit to be free, and not competent to conduct governmental affairs, *because of his inferiority;* and therefore slavery is his doom, and the best condition for him. You might as well say that your rose-bushes and geraniums, in the cellar during winter months, can never bloom because all winter long they have not bloomed. Let the showers of May and sunshine of June caress them, and your opinions will be changed. There is vitality in the human soul. Let the favor of freedom and the power of the gospel shine into it, and God's image will be found daguerreotyped there. We conclude that the destiny of the Negro in this country is to be relieved from prejudice and delivered from bondage.

Doubtless he is unfit now, as a whole, to undertake the administration of the affairs of government. It is, also, not possible, neither is it desirable, that the blacks and whites should be amalgamated. Nor is it admissible that the blacks should ever take part in the administration of our municipal or national affairs. The two races cannot co-exist on an equality. The ultimate destiny of the masses of the Negroes, when they shall have been liberated and trained for it, will be a country, and home, and government of their own. Some will find their way to Africa; some to the West Indies; some may, ere many years, by the advice and help of our Government, and with their own consent, be set up as a colony, under the fostering care of the people of the United States, whose wealth and power their labor has so greatly contributed to promote.

In the meantime, as one of the nearer results of this great war, we shall probably find them in our houses as domestic servants, for which position their fidelity and gentle natures are admirably adapted. These families will be schools where they may be qualifying themselves for the responsibilities of domestic life and the duties of citizenship. These families will aid them, and become, in a certain sense, patrons to them, as they pass out and away to the homes which will be awaiting them. Their labor will still, for a long while, be needed North and South. The tenure of that labor will, in due time, be changed, as sure as the gospel is true and mighty. While the change is taking place as to the kind of domestic service, those now in that position will find their way into the raising of silk, and the cultivation of the vine, and tending the loom, and, perhaps, the cotton-fields of Southern Illinois. These changes may be looked for. I may not prove a true prophet in this. But one thing is certain, viz., the Curse of Noah upon Canaan will not blight the Negro to the end of time ; for long before the end of time Ethiopia will stretch forth her unshackled hands unto God.

Let me, before relieving your already too-severely taxed attention, remind you that "there is a moral bondage, the most galling and degrading species of servitude, in which he may be held, as with chains of brass, who scorns to call any man master on earth. * * * * Those who may have most profoundly investigated the whole question of civil and polical liberty may yet be slaves." Jesus said, "Whosoever committeth sin is the servant of sin." Says Seneca, "One is in bondage to lust, another to avarice, another to ambition." "To be a slave to the passions," says Pythagoras, "is more grievous than to be a slave to tyrants." "Count no one free," says Plato, "who is intent on the indulgence of wicked passions." "All wicked men," says Cicero, "are slaves." "Slavery to sin is true slavery; it is that which degrades, which renders man unfit for the improvement of his nature, the soci-

ety of angels, and the favor of God." "There is a freedom
which is the end and glory of a man." It is freedom from the
condemnation, the power, and the consequences of sin. *This,*
it is Christ's prerogative alone to give. "He is the freeman
whom the truth makes free, and all are slaves besides." Stand
fast in this liberty.

www.ingramcontent.com/pod-product-compliance
Lightning Source LLC
Chambersburg PA
CBHW031823090426
42739CB00008B/1383